Sea Soul JOURNAL

A GUIDED JOURNEY

Insights, Rituals
and Mindful Practices
to Connect with the
Healing Power of the Ocean

PIPPA BEST

WELBECK
BALANCE

Published in 2023 by Welbeck Balance

An imprint of Welbeck Non-Fiction Limited

Part of Welbeck Publishing Group

Offices in: London – 20 Mortimer Street, London W1T 3JW &

Sydney – 205 Commonwealth Street, Surry Hills 2010

www.welbeckpublishing.com

Design and layout © Welbeck Non-Fiction Ltd 2023

Text © Pippa Best 2023

ISBN

978-1-80129-301-3

Typeset by Steve Williams Creative

Printed in Leo Paper Group in Heshan, China

10 9 8 7 6 5 4 3 2 1

Note/Disclaimer

Ever and always,
my deepest gratitude to the sea.

CONTENTS

INTRODUCTION

Rise and Reflect

TRAVEL WITH THE TIDES

High Tide: Self-Compassion

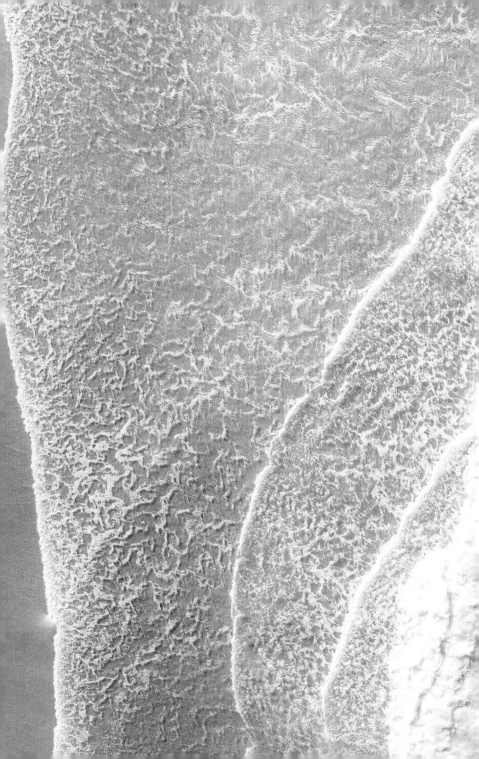

INTRODUCTION

INTO THE SEA

Do you dream of the sea? Or do you head to the ocean when you need space to think, to replenish, to make a change or let go? Whether we stand at the water's edge in awe or visit it in our dreams, the sea lifts and guides us. It is a vast shimmering mystery that connects us all; a universal elixir to restore wholeness and faith, soothe sorrow, clear horizons and open hearts. By the sea, our sea souls awaken. And for sea souls, the ocean is hope, healing and home.

Covering over 70 per cent of our planet, the sea provides much of the oxygen in the air that we breathe, serves as a global thermostat, and nurtures a multitude of carbon-capturing life forms that protect the planet for all. It offers us space to rest, work and play, and sustains us with food. But it also supports us at a deeper emotional level. Intuitively, we sense the healing power of the ocean environment. We know that here, we will always find a fresh perspective: a more fluid understanding of ourselves and our challenges.

Being in and around the sea – or bringing it to mind with images, words and activities like those you'll find here – activates our "blue mind". Wallace J. Nichols, marine biologist, researcher and author of the book *Blue Mind*, explains: "The term 'blue mind' describes the mildly meditative state we fall into when near, in, on, or under water." He notes: "It's the antidote to what we refer to as 'red mind,' which is the anxious, over-connected, and over-stimulated state that defines the new normal of modern life." In a "blue mind" state, we feel calmer, happier, more connected and creative.

To help your mind transition from red to blue, this journal uses imagery, ocean-inspired words, writing prompts, mindful practices and healing sea rituals. It guides you on a journey that will enable you to apply the wisdom of the sea to your daily life, helping you to overcome challenges, embrace change and be in the present.

My hope is that you can use this journal wherever you are, whether you're by the sea or far from the water, longing for the ocean. Allow it to soothe and inspire you – mind, body and sea soul. To awaken your intuition and make space for transformation. To deepen your connection to the water and stimulate change.

About Me

The sea is my muse, my mentor and my medicine. Sea swimming, meditation, journaling, self-compassion, rituals and ocean mindfulness have changed my life (and work) for the better in every way – physically, mentally and spiritually.

As the founder of the nature wellness company Sea Soul Blessings, I have a passion for creating simple, compassionate resources that connect us to the sea – and more deeply to ourselves. In this journal, I share some of the practices I use in my coaching work, at coastal retreats in Cornwall, and within The Sea Circle, my online ocean community. I explore similar Themes here to those in my Sea Soul Journeys Oracle cards and Sea Soul Blessings cards – and you can combine the cards and this journal to take you deeper into these.

I know that mindful activities such as journaling can be life-changing, because I've spent more than 25 years asking writers, coaching clients and retreat attendees questions that prompt deep insight. As well as being a trained life coach, I'm an accredited Blue Health Coach™ – a practice that combines the healing power of nature and "blue spaces" (such as the coast) with elements of traditional life coaching, applied neuroscience, philosophy and more.

Now, more than ever, we need nature's presence and guidance to help enact positive change within us. Change that travels on into our wider communities.

As you use the prompts, tools and practices described in this journal to support and guide you gently through transformation, I hope that you'll build your capacity not just to embrace ebb and flow – but to care for yourself, for others and the natural world that sustains us all. For in healing the sea, we heal ourselves.

To find out more about my journey, discover other ocean-inspired products and a community of sea-lovers, and access free meditations and sea sounds to deepen your experience of this journal, visit www.SeaSoulBlessings.com, or follow me @SeaSoulBlessings on social media.

What to Expect

Your Sea Soul Journal is a space in which to be lifted by the ocean as you move forward toward change, wave by wave. Each wave guides you gently onward via written prompts and ocean practices that invite the sea's wisdom into your life.

Rise and Reflect

You'll start your journey with the Sunrise over the Sea ritual (page 26), which will help you to set an intention to explore a particular area or aspect of your life. As you continue to use your journal, you'll pause to reflect on your progress with the Moonrise over the Sea ritual (page 38).

Themes and Tides

Your journal will guide you through four powerful Themes inspired by the ocean: *Self-Compassion*, *Letting Go*, *Moving Forward* and *Gratitude and Awe*. Each Theme is aligned to a phase of the tide cycle that embodies a similar quality and energy:

High Tide: *Self-Compassion*

Ebbing Tide: *Letting Go*

Low Tide: *Moving Forward*

Rising Tide: *Gratitude and Awe*

Just like our breath, the tides offer a reassuring reminder of life's constant fluidity. As each lesson you learn from the sea flows into the next, turned and polished like sea glass, tide by tide.

In each Theme, you'll find an image, an ocean mantra, a poem and a short piece of writing to help you visualize the sea. Each of these can evoke the ocean and its wisdom within you.

Ocean Qualities

Within each of the Themes, you'll explore three of the ocean's most transformative Ocean Qualities. Each Ocean Quality offers a fresh way to connect with the sea's wisdom and to move forward toward the intention you identified when you began.

For every Ocean Quality, you'll find an empowering affirmation, a compassionate ocean blessing, and a five-minute activity to help you to "Dip a Toe" into that Quality. If you wish, you can then "Dive Deeper" into a written journal prompt and an additional practice (such as a Mindful Practice or an Ocean Ritual) to deepen your understanding and inspire you further.

The Ripple Effect

When you use the practices within this journal and listen to your intuition, you'll gradually awaken the ocean's wisdom within yourself. As this wisdom ripples into your life, you'll find a fresh perspective on challenges, embody the sea's lessons, and take inspired action toward change, always guided by the sea.

Time with the ocean will more deeply connect you to the shifting tides that remind you of your own capacity for change: for releasing and starting anew. And as this tidal flow connects you to the truth that celestial bodies far beyond us move our oceans, you'll begin to access greater awe and gratitude, and develop an appreciation of life's extraordinary everyday gifts.

Sea-inspired Activities

Just like a beach glittering with beachcombing treasure, this journal offers many different ways to soothe yourself, find inspiration and connect with the sea. Use these tools individually to meet a particular need, or combine them to inspire deeper change.

Mantras, Blessings and Affirmations

Each Theme chapter includes a short mantra, an ocean blessing and an affirmation, helping you to call in the sea. For centuries, mantras have been used to connect to the most sacred of universal forces. Repeating mantras can bring inspiration and calm. They can transform how we feel, clearing our minds and redirecting powerful energies – like those of the sea.

The words we speak most often to ourselves also create pathways in our brains that influence how we think, much like repeated waves can forge new channels through sandstone: paths that the sea learns to travel over time. Repeating ocean blessings aloud can encourage you to speak to yourself with kindness and self-compassion, while affirmations can motivate you toward greater self-belief.

Visualizations

Visualizing ourselves by the sea can be mentally and physically soothing, drawing us away from our everyday worries. Even just mindfully reading about the sea can quickly transport us to the water.

The Rise and Reflect practices and each Theme include a short descriptive passage to practice imagining an ocean scene. Just like repeating meaningful words, revisiting a visualization can deepen its impact.

As you read, take time to absorb the images, using all of your senses to bring them to life in your mind and body. You might even like to make your own recording, and then listen to this with your eyes closed.

Journal Prompts

Writing about our thoughts and experiences helps us to release and reduce stress, process emotions, and identify patterns that we might like to change. Regular journaling can also boost resilience and self-acceptance, and improve our overall health.

Use the journal prompts to reflect and consider the changes you want to make from a new perspective. Trust that as you write, you'll tune in to the wisdom of your own intuition, and that of the sea.

"Dip a Toe" Practices

Setting ourselves small achievable goals makes it more likely that we'll move toward change. And just like throwing a pebble into calm waters, the briefest of actions can have a powerful ripple effect.

This is why you'll find short practices to introduce you to each of the Ocean Qualities explored within each Theme. These five-minute practices can be used on their own, or as mindful preparation for the journal prompts that follow.

"Dive Deeper" Practices

When we decide to go deeper, our focus is clear and we experience more impactful benefits. When you make more space available for your journey, your experience of each Ocean Quality's wisdom will be more nuanced and insightful.

Under each Ocean Quality, you will find additional practices that invite you to evolve your understanding: a mixture of mindful exercises, intuitive rituals, and guided journaling sequences.

Mindful Practices

Regular mindfulness reshapes our brain and makes it function more effectively. We become more able to clear our busy "red mind" of stressful thoughts, and our wellbeing improves.

So let reading this journal be a mindful practice in itself. Give yourself space to soak up its content. To breathe. To be with the sea. Then go deeper into some of the mindful practices here – a mix of breathwork, self-compassion, creative play and movement.

Ocean Rituals

We use rituals to honour and acknowledge the significance of particular moments or milestones, to shape our identity and culture, and make meaning of our lives. Historically, rituals have given humans a sense of belonging – and often rooted us in nature.

Use the opening Sunrise over the Sea and Moonrise over the Sea rituals to awaken the ocean within you, honouring each fresh beginning and lesson learned. The additional rituals in each Theme will guide you toward a more sacred connection to the sea and your inner knowing.

Let the rituals in this journal inform your journey in whatever way feels true to you – as a devotional practice, to call in magic, as an intuitive process to gather inspiration, or simply as another way to be mindful. As you reflect on these experiences, allow your inner wisdom to rise up and flow through these pages, rippling out the ocean's light.

And Remember...

As you explore the practices in this journal, listen carefully to your body and pay attention to your own physical and emotional needs. If you have any existing medical conditions, or are pregnant, seek expert advice before trying any of the physical activities or breathing practices shared here. Always tend gently to yourself.

How to Get the Most Out of Your Journal

To deepen the benefits of time spent with this journal, use the following simple practices to shape your approach, and to make the sea a more constant presence in your life.

Start with an Ocean Mindset

Be the sea. Open your awareness up as wide as the ocean, and let the possibilities be vast and endless, free of judgement and expectation. Swim deep into your intuition. To find your flow, be guided by your own cycles, rhythm and pace.

Set a Clear Intention – and Revisit Often

At the start of your journey with this journal, use Sunrise over the Sea (page 26) to invite in the sea's guidance, and to identify a specific change you would like to make in your life – large or small. If you wish, each morning – or every time you use your journal – you can revisit this ritual or its journal prompts to strengthen your intention, deepen your connection, and identify the next step to move you closer to your goal.

Regularly revisiting your intention in this way will help you to find greater clarity, motivation and focus, and deepen the benefits of the other practices in this book.

Reflect Regularly on Your Journey

To inspire you onward, make time to pause and reflect on your progress often. To get the most out of your journey here, use the Moonrise over the Sea practice (page 38) to reflect with compassion on your progress and gather insights. Notice what has changed, and what you have learnt.

You can use this ritual and its journal prompts each evening, on each full moon, or each time you complete a session with your journal.

Evoke the Sea with All Your Senses

Use the oceanic images and descriptions to imagine yourself in or by the water. What can you feel, see, smell, touch and taste? Sense the colours, textures, details and physical experience of time spent by the sea.

Try playing sea sounds as you journal, or meditate with the Ocean Breath practice (see page 30) to listen to the sea within. Ocean sounds can make you feel more compassionate and connected – to others, to yourself and to nature. Reawakening ancient neural maps in your brain that associate the sounds of water (or of the womb) with security and sustenance, they support you to relax, heal and replenish.

Watching films of the sea can also reduce anxiety and pain, and evoke positive memories. You can find free audio recordings of ocean sounds, meditations, videos and images at my website: www.seasoulblessings.com.

Bring the Ocean into Your Home

Create a space at home where you can regularly pause and bring the ocean to mind. You might create an ocean altar, or use a small display of sea treasures, images, gifts and colours that evoke the sea. Place your journal somewhere you'll see it often.

Embrace New Horizons

Stimulate your creativity, engage your brain and expand your sense of what's possible by trying new things and expanding your comfort zone. Explore a wide range of ocean practices and approaches to connecting with the sea, and try different ways of using your journal.

Ways to Journey

There are as many different ways to work with the practices in these pages as there are moods of the sea. You could create a regular daily, weekly or monthly journal practice and work through each Theme and Ocean Quality in sequence. Or simply call on the sea's insight when you need it.

Let your inner knowing shape your journey as the waves shape the shore, uncovering fresh tools to support and inspire you in each moment. Here are a few suggestions to get you started.

An Intuitive Dive

Tune in to your intention with Sunrise over the Sea (page 26), then let your intuition guide you to any page or section of the journal. Dip into whatever practices you find there.

By Theme

Let your energy or particular need guide your focus.

- If you're feeling self-critical, fill your own cup with the prompts and practices in High Tide: Self-Compassion (page 52).
- If there's something you want to release, try Ebbing Tide: Letting Go (page 90).
- If you're feeling stuck, visit Low Tide: Moving Forward (page 128).
- If you're feeling low, let Rising Tide: Gratitude and Awe boost your mood (page 166).

By Ocean Quality

There are three Ocean Qualities within each Theme:

Present (page 60)
Enough (page 74)
Expansive (page 82)

Curious (page 136)
Stretch (page 150)
Persist (page 158)

Courage (page 98)
Heard (page 112)
Space (page 120)

Receive (page 174)
Play (page 188)
Magic (page 196)

If one of these resonates, dive straight into that. For example: When you're feeling afraid, turn to Courage. When you're distracted and overwhelmed, visit Present. When you want to reach toward a new goal, explore Stretch. When you want to be creative, enjoy Play.

By Journal Prompts

If you wish, you can focus solely on the written journal prompts, working through these in sequence and using them to identify your goals and record your responses and experiences.

By Mindful Practice or Ritual

You may want to choose a practice or ritual that meets an immediate need, or that you wish to explore or revisit. Use these to deepen your capacity for mindfulness or your connection to your intuitive sea soul:

Mindful Practices
- Ocean Breath – *breathing* (page 30)
- From the Ocean, For the Ocean – *self-compassion* (page 80)
- Deep Sighs – *breathing* (page 118)
- Mexican Wave – *somatic* (page 156)
- Ocean Art – *creative* (page 194)
- Tidal Breaths – *breathing* (page 42)

Ocean Rituals
- A ritual to set an intention: Sunrise over the Sea (page 32)
- A ritual to reflect and renew: Moonrise over the Sea (page 44)
- A ritual to journey within and without: Sand Spiral (page 88)
- A ritual to create space: Beach Clearing (page 126)
- A ritual to inspire perseverance: Sea Glass, the Sea and Me (page 164)
- A ritual to awaken your ocean magic: Ocean Energy Flow (page 202)

By Mantra, Blessing or Affirmation

Use your ocean mantras, blessings and affirmations to ground you in moments of challenge, or repeat them as part of a regular meditation or chanting practice. Focus on a single affirmation or blessing that inspires you, or use a series of mantras or affirmations as the basis for an empowering meditation. Alternatively, create a regular self-compassion practice by reading each blessing aloud to yourself.

By Ocean Visualization

Sometimes you just want to be transported to the sea. In those moments, select one of the six written visualizations, and spend a few minutes sensing yourself there at the ocean's edge.

- Into the Sunrise Sea (page 34)
- Full Moon Rising (page 47)
- The Stone Steps (page 57)
- Storm Watcher (page 95)
- Beachcomber (page 133)
- Summer Shores (page 171)

Use Ocean Oracle or Blessings Cards

If you have the Sea Soul Journeys Oracle or Blessings cards, use these to guide you to a particular Theme or Ocean Quality; or combine your journal practice with an oracle reading to deepen your understanding of each prompt.

Return Like the Sea

Keep reusing this journal and revisiting its prompts to find new answers. Do the same activity every day for a week and see what appears. Focus on a new intention, challenge or area of life you wish to change, and start all over again. Add layers to the journal with each use, or keep a separate notebook and transfer your prompts there.

Create Your Own Ocean Retreat

Take this journal and its practices to the sea. Start your journal session with a real ocean sunrise, or if conditions allow, end it with a moonlit swim. Alternatively, host an ocean-inspired retreat at home, using the practices and rituals described in these pages.

RISE AND REFLECT

Discover how to begin and complete each
journal practice, deepening your journey with
regular ocean check-ins.

Set an Intention

SUNRISE OVER THE SEA

SALTED

Those who dip in the sea

to start the day

are not nuts.

They just feel more

ready, salted.

Swimming in the sea at sunrise paints the day with possibility. It stops time, even as it makes you achingly aware of change, second by glorious second. For a brief moment, magic is visible. And you have a deep soul knowing that you – yes, you – are part of this beauty. You are a tuning fork resonating with wonder. You are sure of what matters and why. You let go. You step into the flow. Your intention is clear.

The truth is, of course, that you are always full of possibility. Every breath you take offers you a fresh start – a new sunrise over the sea, and the opportunity to set a clear intention for the day ahead. Deep down, you already know what needs to change. You just need to create space to tune in to that; to trust that the ocean will support and strengthen you on your journey; and to listen deeply to your sea soul's guidance.

The Sunrise over the Sea ritual combines the mindful practice of ocean breathing with a sea visualization to help you to connect with your ocean intuition. Once you have made that connection, the questions and journal prompts guide you to identify a change you want to make – large or small. That change becomes your intention. And you can use the ocean blessing and affirmation to encourage you toward that.

You might have already identified the change you want to make. If not, you can use the ritual on page 32 to set a clear intention as you begin your journey. Then revisit the ritual or journal prompts each morning to identify your next small step toward that, strengthening your intention.

Blessing
May you embrace change and flow.

Affirmation
As the sea, I am always changing.

Mindful Practice
Ocean Breath (*Ujjayi Pranayama*)

In this practice, which originates in yoga, your breath evokes the sound of the sea, calming your nervous system and clearing your mind. Use Ocean Breath by itself as a mindful practice, or at the start of the Sunrise over the Sea ritual, below. Ocean Breath can also be used to prepare for meditation or while moving through yoga poses. It can bring the sea to you whenever you need it.

In yoga, we connect to and cultivate *prana* or life-force energy – an energy that runs through all natural things, including us. It's easy to sense that *prana* by a roaring sea, with negative ions crackling in the air. More often, though, we're busy and distracted, and don't sense the energy within and around us. This practice is a powerful way to bring your attention to your senses and to *prana* in just a few minutes.

The calming sound of your breath activates your body's vagus nerve – just like cold water dips do – instigating a state of restful vitality as your parasympathetic nervous system takes charge.

The internal movement of your breath massages your organs, stimulates the digestive system, and generates internal heat. Ocean Breath also helps to relieve sinus pressure and headaches, and improves sleep quality. It also helps to relieve sinus pressure and headaches, and improves sleep quality.

Try this practice standing, lying down or sitting up with a straight back.

Spend a little time breathing in and out through your mouth, bringing your attention to your breath.

Begin to deepen the breath, so that it becomes louder. As you breathe in, deeply fill your lungs, slowly and steadily, and lift your chest. As you breathe out, release the air with an audible sigh, allowing your belly to relax completely. Take time to finish each exhalation. You might also like to take a short pause at the end of every exhale before repeating the cycle.

Once you've found a rhythm, close your mouth – but continue to breathe in the same way. Your body naturally adjusts so that you're breathing in and out through your nose, but you can still hear the "haaaa" sound of the breath that echoes the sound of the sea. Surrender to the sound and rhythm of your breathing.

Close your eyes and spend a couple of minutes breathing in this way, listening to the sound of the ocean in your breath. You might imagine waves rolling up on the shore, and drawing out again – just as your breath does.

When you're ready, return to a normal breathing pattern.

Taking just a few ocean breaths can have a powerful soothing effect. It's an energizing way to clear your mind and relax your body so that you can make more considered decisions. After a couple of minutes, you can step into your day feeling grounded and calm, having awoken that ocean of *prana* within, or move on to set an intention with the Sunrise over the Sea ritual.

Ocean Ritual
To Set an Intention: Sunrise over the Sea

This ritual will support you to identify a guiding intention.
One that can inspire an intuitive and impactful journaling practice,
and steer you clearly through the activities in this journal –
mind, body and sea soul.

*Begin with Ocean Breath (page 30) to calm your
mind and connect you to the sea.*

*Close your eyes and imagine the ocean in the moments
before the sunrise. You could use the visualization, on page 34,
or meditate on the image above on pages 26–27.*

*Alternatively, try to sense the kind of physical sensations or emotions
you would feel when waiting on the beach for the sun to rise. Or use
writing, drawing or another creative practice to connect you to the
scene. The aim is to shape this ritual in whatever way best supports
you to bring the experience of an ocean sunrise to life.*

*Gently allow your breathing to return to normal, and begin to
imagine the moment when the sun rises above the horizon. Pause
to sense into the clarity, transformation and wonder of an ocean
sunrise, and invite the sea to guide you forward.*

As you imagine the sun rippling out to touch you across the sea, ask: **What do I want to change?**

You might find your attention drawn to a particular element of the ocean scene, receive a visit from a messenger of some kind, or hear or see a word, sign or symbol. You might pause to draw an oracle card, or simply answer this question in your mind.

Listen to your sea soul. **What's pulling at your heart right now? What clarity lies within? What new start is possible?**

When you're ready, use your answer to form your intention, naming a change that you want to move toward. Speak it aloud: **From this moment onward, I move toward . . .**

If you have already set an intention and are revisiting this ritual each morning, take a moment to reclaim your original intention here.

Next, identify a small action that can move you toward that bigger change: **The first step I will take toward that today is . . .**

Place a hand on your heart. Take a few final deep ocean breaths and imagine filling yourself up with all that the sunrise over the sea can offer you. Give thanks to the sea.

Bring yourself back to the present moment and use the journal prompts on pages 36–37 to capture your answers to the questions above – and to put your intention in writing. Then step into your day, and this journal, with a clear intention as your guide.

Visualization
Into the Sunrise Sea

*The gulls are quiet: dark checkmarks against a pale
slate of early morning sky. Yet you stomp silently on, barely awake.
Heading toward that hint of indigo beyond.*

*You can already taste the unmistakable tang of the air, salt whisked
around the coast like a knowing whisper. As the birds call loudly to
each other, impatient for the day to begin.*

*Now, a line of pale light cracks slowly, a wry smile on the horizon.
And the sky pinks, blending crimson and purple.*

*Travelling onward, your boots judder over slipping pebbles.
Oystercatchers scattering, peeping and looping. Dark water reflected
in your eyes, betraying the fear in your gut. But even on land,
a thickening current guides you onward.*

*A white egret rises, wings hooping at half speed as you peel
off your layers. Goosebumps lifting from your skin like goose
barnacles on driftwood.*

Gulls ascend in a crowd, fighting over sprats and swooping through invisible thermals, as you pause, half in, half out of your clothes. Struck still and silent by the gold of the sun as it eases itself up from beneath the edge of the world with quiet aplomb. Before tipping itself into the sea, and rolling out a glittering rug of rippling silver that curls toward you.

The sun rises, huge and hopeful, toward the sky. As you pull off the last of your clothing, a tingling warmth grazes your skin.

Moons before you were aware of it, this path was laid for you. Long before you woke, your feet had begun to walk you here. And now the way glitters ahead: a partner calling you to dance.

The first step toward the sea is followed by the second. And the third. You are ready before you are ready. Your path is clear. And into the water you go.

Journal Prompts

From this moment onward, what do I want to change?

_____

_____

_____

_____

_____

_____

_____

_____

_____

_____

_____

_____

_____

_____

_____

_____

_____

_____

_____

And what is my first step toward this?

Reflect and Renew

MOONRISE OVER THE SEA

NIGHT SWIM

Woven in by phosphorescence

on a moon-spun ocean night,

I am guided by the tingle,

stitched through undulating light,

rolled in folds of boundless fabric,

beyond knowing or delight.

I am lost in the unravel

and then sewn back, eyes eel-bright.

atching the moon rise over the ocean connects us to magic, mystery and awe. It reminds us of the beauty and power of inward reflection; of ritual, cycles and transformation. It calls us to find the light in the dark; to follow a rippling silver path toward the unknown.

The Moonrise over the Sea ritual combines the mindful practice of Tidal Breaths with a sea visualization to connect to your ocean intuition. The questions and journal prompts then guide you to gather insights and reflect on your progress.

Use the Moonrise over the Sea ritual or journal prompts any time you want to sense your movement toward change, deepen your ocean connection, ground yourself in the practice of compassionate reflection, or reaffirm your commitment to your intention. Use the affirmation and ocean blessing to support and empower you on your journey.

The moonrise reminds us that even in the darkest moments – when it feels like we have stalled or reversed – the moon and tides are turning. However you feel, taking the time to reflect and renew allows the sea to gently move you forward.

Revisit this ritual as you approach the end of your journey with this journal. Turn the pages to witness all that you have uncovered, experienced, released and appreciated. Reconnect to ever-renewing cycles of beginnings and endings, day and night, light and dark – to life's continuous onward movement. Let the rippling ocean moonlight remind you that every change leads to another opportunity to expand and stretch. What is next?

Blessing

May each wave move you forward with grace and hope.

Affirmation

I celebrate and learn from each wave that guides me forward.

Mindful Practice
Tidal Breaths

In this grounding breathing practice, you will combine circular breathing with mantras and ocean visualizations.

The circular (or box) breath is a breathing pattern used by yogis, singers, doctors, athletes and the armed forces alike to find calm, reduce feelings of stress, and reach a heightened state of concentration and focus. Here, you will also be nourished by mantras that highlight your inner resources and your place in life's constantly changing cycles.

Whenever you want to reconnect to the lessons of this journal, use these mantras – with or without the circular breathing – as a reminder that even in moments of pause, release or retreat, you are always in flow, always moving forward.

Take a moment to relax, ground your feet on the floor, and bring your attention to your breath. Imagine yourself standing or sitting by the seashore.

Breathe in for a count of four. Hold your breath in for a count of four. Breathe out for a count of four. Hold your breath out for a count of four. Repeat.

As you breathe, you might like to visualize the shifting tides, or a single wave rolling in and out. Breathe in as the tide rises, and out as it falls. As you hold your breath in between, imagine the waves reaching their highest or lowest point of momentary stillness.

Once you are comfortable with the pacing and rhythm of your breath, try replacing the counting with mantras:

As you breathe in, fill your lungs and feel your heart swell:
I am thankful.

As you hold, sense the compassion in your heart:
I feel compassion.

As you breathe out, enjoy the release in your body:
And I let go.

As you hold, feel the space and clarity within you:
I move forward.

After a few minutes, return to a normal breathing pattern.

Taking just a few Tidal Breaths can have a powerful soothing and clarifying effect. The more regularly you practise, the more your brain associates this type of breathing – and these mantras – with calm, clarity and a deeper connection to the sea.

Use Tidal Breaths as a standalone practice, or to clear your mind and attune to the sea as you prepare for the Moonrise over the Sea ritual.

Ocean Ritual
To Reflect and Renew: Moonrise over the Sea

This ritual will create space for you to pause and absorb the insights that arise as you use your journal; and encourage you to witness and appreciate your progress.

Begin with Tidal Breaths (see page 42) to calm and connect you to the ocean's cycles, flow and wisdom. When you're ready, gently allow your breathing to return to normal.

Close your eyes and imagine the moonrise over the water, using all of your senses. You might use the visualization on page 47 or bring your focus to the image on pages 38–39; feel into the physical sensations or emotions; or use another creative practice to bring the scene to life for you. Trust that however you experience this, you are connecting to the moon and the sea in the right way for you.

Sense the ocean's effect on you. Connect to your ocean intuition, and invite the sea to guide you forward. Ask: **What has changed?**

Listen to whatever arises.

You might simply observe your thoughts, without judgement; become curious about where your attention is being drawn (and the meaning of this); or seek out a symbol, sign or messenger within the ocean scene.

Pause to acknowledge your progress toward your intention. Offer yourself loving kindness for each small step forward, even if this is simply a desire to change, a new awareness of your experiences, or time spent using this journal.

Remind yourself that even the tiniest of shifts creates ripples. Notice that even when you feel stuck, there is always something to learn. Ask: **What have I learnt?**

Place a hand on your heart. Take a few final Tidal Breaths, and give thanks to the ocean: in the struggles, the challenges and the changes, you are not alone. The sea is always holding you.

Bring your attention back to the present moment, and capture any insights using the journal prompts on pages 48–49.

Visualization
Full Moon Rising

The day sighs softly as it fades from the sky. The last pinks of the passing sun linger as they are washed from the west. To the east, a smear of grey cloud thins above the hills, wisps of yellow-edged nets drawn before glimpses of a rising moon.

As the clouds drift into dark corners of the sky, the moon dusts the sea a silver green. Moonlight stirs shaky lines through the waves, as if the ocean's mineral depths were glowing, moss and luminous lichen breathing life into cracks in a vast temple wall. Lessons unrolled as a mercurial scroll that stretches far into the darkness.

*Tomorrow's path glimmers through the undulating jade.
Not always visible, but unmistakably there.*

The backs of seagulls catch white as they fly into the shadows, seeking open water to settle. While the moon, at first impossibly huge on the horizon, rises to become a perfect white pebble rolled onto a vast dark beach. A tiny source of immense power, pulling the tides, wave by wave.

Journal Prompts

What has changed?

_____

_____

_____

_____

_____

_____

_____

_____

_____

_____

_____

_____

_____

_____

_____

_____

_____

_____

_____

_____

_____

And what have I learnt on this journey so far?

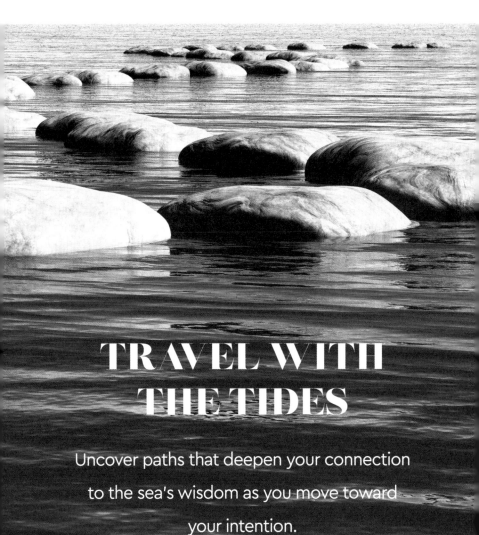

TRAVEL WITH THE TIDES

Uncover paths that deepen your connection to the sea's wisdom as you move toward your intention.

HIGH TIDE
Self Compassion

OCEAN MANTRA:

All that I seek in the sea flows freely within me.

FRIENDSHIP

The sea listens.

She doesn't question,

fix, judge or moan.

Just rocks me gently,

makes salt of my tears.

Lifts me, and carries me home.

HIGH TIDE

At high tide, the sea is closest to the shore. An ocean of compassion lies within touching distance. There is barely a moment to question your calling; no vast beach to cross before stepping into the liminal space of change. Just one step and you immerse – beyond resistance, held in the ocean's tender caress.

Self-Compassion

Pioneering self-compassion researcher Dr Kristin Neff identifies three core elements of a self-compassion practice. These are mindfulness (being present with our emotions and experiences), self-kindness (being kind to ourselves) and common humanity (being aware of our suffering as a shared human experience). The sea offers you opportunities to seek out all three.

Time spent in, around or inspired by the sea can become a powerful act of self-care and kindness. The immediacy of the ocean's movement brings you into the present, away from fear and regret, while the awe you feel at the water's edge connects you to something greater than yourself. All the way to the horizon, the sea holds space for you. And as you journal here, you can hold that ocean space for yourself.

Let this journal be a place in which you can simply be as you are, do what you want, and feel whatever you feel, without judgement or expectation. Where you can set the boundaries of the experience you want to have, listen to your truths, tend to your needs, and leave clearer about what matters. Where you treat yourself with kindness as you face challenges and move toward change, speaking to yourself as you would to a loved one.

As the high tide sea holds and soothes you – mind, body and sea soul – gently begin to shift the way you motivate and care for yourself. Allow your inner critic and chattering doubts to quieten.

Allow this first tidal Theme to guide you into the present moment; to encourage you to treat yourself with self-kindness (knowing that you are enough just as you are); and to seek out a more expansive perspective on your struggles. One that connects you to others, and reminds you that you are never alone.

Blessing

May the sea hold you tenderly, as you hold yourself.

Visualization
The Stone Steps

At high tide, heavy granite steps lead straight into the sea: a reassuringly sturdy path into nature's own vast infinity pool. This is where you head when you need to be held. By the rock beneath your feet. And by the water.

On rough days, you sit at the top of the stairs and sense the whoosh of the swell crashing against the steps. The ocean rising up and sucking away: a noisy matador flicking its wild white cape at the shore. Watching seal pups play between the peaks, your emotions slowly settle.

On calm days, you are lulled by gurgling sounds that emerge as tiny fish from the gaps between the stones. Soothed by rippling kelp forests and the undulations of jellyfish. Guided by sleek dark cormorants diving fathoms down in search of darting shoals of sand eels, mullet and mackerel.

Walking into the arms of the sea, you are lifted and embraced.

Affirmation

I tend to myself with compassion, held by the sea.

Journal Prompts

Reflect upon your own experience of self-compassion and kindness. If you find it hard to offer these to yourself, consider what a dear friend might suggest you do to support yourself as you move toward your intention.

How can I support myself on this journey?

_____

_____

_____

_____

_____

_____

_____

_____

_____

_____

_____

_____

_____

And what can I do to support myself today?

_____

_____

_____

_____

_____

_____

_____

_____

_____

_____

_____

_____

_____

_____

_____

_____

_____

Present

*The sea is a constant reviver,
a whole-body sensation pulling you into
the now. It calls you into this breath.
Into this wave. Into this thrill and this leap.
Into your presence. It sounds the pulse
of your soul, urging you to claim
this entire being.*

A s the Zen master Thich Nhat Hanh once said, "The past is gone, the future is not yet here, and if we do not go back to ourselves in the present moment, we cannot be in touch with life."

The ocean calls you into the immediacy of your existence. With the vastness of the view. A blast of sea spray on your skin. The tang of salt and seaweed on the air. Stepping into a cold sea, you are utterly and completely here. In your body. In the water. In your life.

Bringing the ocean to mind when you're far from the sea can also shift you into a more meditative state. One that allows you to experience this moment, here and now, with greater depth and richness.

The first stage of practising self-compassion is this kind of mindfulness – stepping into a deeper awareness of the present moment. This might simply mean pausing to witness what you are feeling, physically and emotionally. As you observe the present moment – with curiosity in place of judgement – you can more clearly identify your most immediate challenges, and explore where and how to offer comfort. You notice the presence of suffering – within you, or without. And that information guides you toward what you most need. A glass of water, a stretch, a rest, to be held or heard?

Only in the present moment can you change, or sense your current challenge clearly. Only here can you hear your intuition, and listen to the messages of the sea, with all your senses. Standing on the water's edge, fully present to the sea within and without, you attune to life's shifting layers of perception. You are between two worlds – air and water, the sea and the land, body and spirit, both your physical experience and a deeper calling or connection to something more.

Blessing
May you be present to all that
arrives on your shores.

Affirmation
I am present to all that flows
around and within me.

DIP A TOE INTO PRESENCE

Bring your attention to the present moment:
What can I see, hear, taste, touch, smell?

*Notice your emotional experience of this present moment,
naming any sensations or emotions:*
What am I feeling right now?

*Identify where you feel these emotions in your body,
without judgement:*
**An ache in your neck, a tense jaw, nausea, shortness of breath,
something else?**

DIVE DEEPER INTO PRESENCE

On this journey, what shifts when
I come into the present?

_____

_____

_____

_____

_____

_____

And how can being present support me today?

_____

_____

_____

_____

_____

_____

_____

Guided Journaling Journey

Read the Theme introduction, and use the "Dip a Toe" activities to bring yourself consciously into the present moment. Then, thinking about any changes you want to make, use the following writing prompts to reflect on your present, past and future influences:

In this present moment, what are the impacts of not making the change I want to make?

_____

_____

_____

_____

_____

_____

_____

_____

_____

_____

_____

_____

_____

_____

What has been my response to this challenge in the past?

_____

_____

_____

_____

_____

_____

_____

How is my past influencing how I respond to this now?

_____

_____

_____

_____

_____

_____

_____

What useful lessons from my past could I
bring into this present moment?

What do I fear about the future if I don't make this change? And if I do?

_____

_____

_____

_____

_____

_____

_____

_____

_____

_____

_____

_____

_____

_____

_____

_____

_____

_____

In what ways is this imagined future influencing how
I respond to making this change now?

When I am focused on neither the past nor the future, but am fully present (in my body, mind and life), what do I know about my current challenge and my capacity to respond to this?

_____

_____

_____

_____

_____

_____

_____

_____

_____

_____

_____

_____

_____

_____

_____

_____

What is my soul urging me to be present to
most of all in this moment?

_____

_____

_____

_____

_____

_____

And what first step could I take toward that today?

_____

_____

_____

_____

_____

_____

_____

_____

Enough

The sea tends to its boundaries. It offers ample opportunity for all, yet is beholden to none. In understanding its innate sufficiency, it releases you of any need to prove your own worth. It invites you to revel in being exactly as you are.

We don't ever question whether the sea has done enough to be worthy of our love. We know that sometimes it rises and sometimes it falls. Sometimes its clarity is stunning, sometimes it's chaotic and unclear. We don't doubt that even on the days when it lacks the energy to lift itself from the floor, colour can be found within.

We love the sea – without asking or expecting it to be anything other than it is. And in connecting to that love, we begin to connect more deeply to our love for others – and for ourselves.

In a culture that encourages us to judge our worth by productivity, it can be hard to feel we are enough. To stop and rest. To release the constant striving. Even when we learn to appreciate all that we have and are, the world can leave us feeling inadequate. But the responsibility of making change in troubled times is ours to share. You don't have to be enough on your own.

When you experience feelings of self-doubt and self-criticism, put unrealistic expectations on yourself, make negative comparisons or unhelpful assumptions, set boundaries that leave you overwhelmed and frustrated . . . pause, breathe and turn your attention to the sea.

Remind yourself to notice and celebrate all that you are doing – and all that you bring to the world, simply by existing. Speak to yourself as you would speak to a dear friend. Ask: *What if I were to appreciate myself as I appreciate the ocean?* Without judgement or expectations, and with an open heart.

Instead of driving yourself forward with criticism, encourage yourself with kindness. It isn't easy to shift a lifetime of conditioning, but regularly practising self-compassion and self-kindness can rewrite the thoughts that make you feel less than enough – like so many waves breaking against the rocks, smoothing them over time.

Blessing

May you know you are worthy of love,
just as you are, just as the sea is.

Affirmation

I am enough, just as I am,
just as the sea is.

DIP A TOE INTO ENOUGH

Take five deep breaths. Notice your body's capacity to breathe in exactly what it needs, and to breathe out what it doesn't.

Offer yourself some soothing touch – a hand on your heart, holding your own hand, a hug, soft strokes on your skin, whatever feels nurturing. Allow yourself to experience how it feels to deeply receive your own loving support.

As a further act of tender self-care, slowly drink a glass of water. Appreciate each sip, feeling your mind and body being nourished.

DIVE DEEPER INTO ENOUGH

On this journey, what shifts if I treat myself as if I am always worthy of love?

_____

_____

_____

_____

_____

_____

And how can I offer myself love today?

_____

_____

_____

_____

_____

_____

_____

Mindful Practice
From the Ocean, For the Ocean

In this practice, you will be visualizing the ocean as a source of
compassion – to receive or replenish, depending on your needs.

Inspired by a self-compassion exercise from Dr Kristin Neff,
in which you breathe compassion in and out, this "compassionate
breaths" practice evokes the sea as its source, as a nurturing force.

Since almost half of the oxygen in our atmosphere is formed by
ocean micro-organisms (phytoplankton), there's actually a good
chance that every other nourishing breath you take really does
come from the sea.

Gauge your capacity and need for compassion in each moment.
Sometimes you'll be able to give more. Sometimes you'll need
to focus on receiving. You can't care for others if you don't first care
for yourself. And there is always enough compassion to draw
from in the sea.

*Close your eyes and bring an image of the sea to mind.
Imagine this as a vast pool of compassion – a source of loving
kindness that connects and nourishes us all.*

*Offer yourself some compassionate touch,
like a hand on your heart or belly.*

*Breathe in "**from the ocean**", and imagine receiving kindness
from the sea. As you continue breathing, allow yourself to feel
more deeply held and supported by each new inhale.*

*Assess how you feel in the present moment. Exhausted by
caring for others? Then continue focusing on your inhale.*

*Feeling stronger? Then add a second element: with each exhale,
breathe out "**for the ocean**", imagining that you are offering
kindness and replenishing the ocean.*

Receive with the inhale, give with the exhale.

*Practise breathing in this way for a few minutes. When you
feel ready, regulate your breath.*

*As you gently go about the rest of your day,
pause and breathe in the ocean's compassion
whenever you need it.*

Expansive

Your body understands that so much of it is simply particles of water – flowing into everything, connecting everything, accepting everything. The horizon is infinite, the depths vast. Your capacity to extend and grow is both inclusive and unlimited.

We spend our first months floating in amniotic fluid. Up to six months of age, we retain ancient reflexes that guide us to swim – a reminder that we are part of something immense and ancient: the oceans. The adult human body is up to 60 per cent water – our brains and lungs even more. Water is vital to our survival. And like love, it flows through everything.

As you float in the sea, you meld with the water. You can imagine your energy moving on beyond your physical edges to connect with the ocean. Feel love flowing from you to the sea and back again. On land, when you need reminding of our interconnectedness, you can imagine and revisit that experience.

In the sea, you can sense that we are all so much more than the constraints of our environment, or the limitations we place on ourselves. Widening your perception, you also begin to recognize our common humanity. That you are not "wrong", "other" or alone. You, alongside so many more, are simply living the human experience, with all its peaks and troughs.

The more you connect to these truths, the more you can change. As you acknowledge shared experiences, these support you to move forward. As you sense your place in a vast ocean of existence, constantly fluid, constantly shifting from one form into another. Connected not just to other humans, but to nature.

Blessing

May you connect to the whole; and find yourself in
the vastness of the water.

Affirmation

I am connected to all: together, we are the ocean.

DIP A TOE INTO EXPANSIVE

Identify three other people who have experienced something similar to your current challenge (you don't have to know them personally).

Then consider how many others have or will experience this challenge, all around the world. Take a moment to imagine all of you connected across the oceans, held and supported by the water.

Place your hand on your heart, and repeat these mantras five times, rippling loving kindness out to yourself and all beings:

May I and all beings be loved.

May I and all beings be nourished.

May I and all beings know the gifts of the sea.

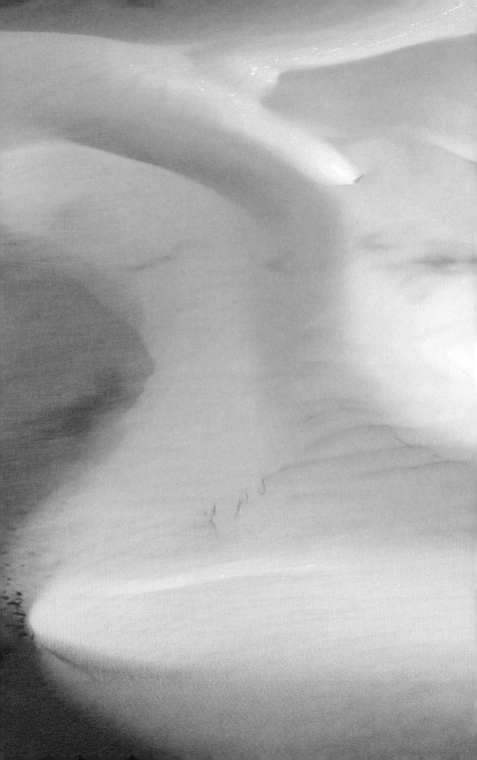

DIVE DEEPER INTO EXPANSIVE

What shifts if I connect to others or widen my
perspective on this journey?

_____

_____

_____

_____

_____

_____

And how could I do that today?

_____

_____

_____

_____

_____

_____

_____

Ocean Ritual
To Journey Within and Without: Sand Spiral

In this ritual, you will create and walk a spiral as you consider
your current challenge.

We find spirals all around us in nature – in the beauty of a whelk,
periwinkle or nautilus seashell, in the curl of a breaking wave or sea
spirals seen from space – even in the structure of our own DNA.
Spirals are often used to represent flow, expansion, cycles of
change, the evolution of consciousness, intuition, mother
goddesses or the feminine, and the mutability of water.

Walking a spiral provides a shift of state and perspective,
not unlike the experience of immersion in water. Walking a spiral
inward, you bring your attention within. Walking outward, your
attention expands. You revisit challenges from new perspectives,
and experience a form of rebirth.

Walking a spiral alongside others can be a powerful ritual to share
– each following their individual journey, yet noticing where your
paths and experiences cross.

State the change you want to make.

*Bring your awareness to the presence of the ocean,
and imagine opening your heart, mind and sea soul
to receive guidance.*

*Starting from the centre, create a spiral large enough to walk
within. You might draw this in the sand, or use objects to mark the
line. If you can't get to the beach, create one elsewhere in nature.
Or draw a spiral and imagine making this journey.*

*As you create your spiral, feel your connection to the unending
flow of the ocean. Sense your capacity to manifest growth
and progression.*

*When you have drawn or created your spiral, revisit your intention
and mindfully walk the path of your spiral inward. As you travel from
the outside in, imagine travelling deeper into what lies at the core of
the change you want to make, coming closer to your truths with
each step. Pay attention to whatever insight comes to you.*

*At the centre, take some time to be still, sensing your inner
world and the ocean's flow all around you.*

*Now mindfully walk the spiral outward. As you do so,
widen your perspective of your challenge, sensing your
capacity to move through and beyond this.*

*Returning to the start of your spiral, offer thanks
to the sea and your intuition. Reflect on the experience in
your journal, or in discussion with a friend.*

EBBING TIDE
Letting Go

OCEAN MANTRA:

The sea can teach us ebb and flow:
to hold an ocean, and let go.

OCEAN EXHALE

I let go

of the fury

of the tears

of the heartache

of the fears.

I let go.

I let go

of exhaustion

of blame

of bitterness

of pain.

I let go.

I let go

of envy

of guilt

of panic.

All is spilt.

I let go.

I let go

and the sea knows.

On she flows.

Like a wave,

I breathe in

and I grow.

To let go.

EBBING TIDE

As the tide releases, it creates space in which to pause, to ebb and reset. There is no longer the full sensory immersion of high tide, nor yet the clarity of low. But here, in the letting go, the edges of hidden truths are slowly revealed, in relief. Little by little, the unknown becomes visible, and new possibilities are glimpsed.

Letting Go

An ancient Zen proverb reminds us that: "Knowledge is learning something every day. Wisdom is letting go of something every day."

The sea is always releasing. At top tide, there is a moment of steadiness, a hiatus before the pull. Sea and shore seem loath to let each other go. For this brief moment, they rest in each other's arms, in the comfort of the familiar. Perhaps resisting not just their separation, but the exposure of what lies beneath: honesty, vulnerability, fear – and the tenderest hope of uncovering unimaginable beauty.

Anemones draw in their tentacles, mussels clench, and glittering fish dart into caves. And then – with a moment of courage and the splintering of one final falling wave – the drawing back and letting go begins. Each release breathes life into the next, allowing a new cycle to take shape, wave by wave.

In this Theme, you are called to release resistance, brave the unknown, change a pattern, make space for the new. To find the courage to let go. To face both loss and hope as you move toward your intention.

When you find the courage to be heard and to release, you slowly reveal a realm of transition, transformation – and all the beautiful in between messiness of that. As the ebbing tide reveals new paths, you make room for fresh possibilities within yourself.

Blessing

May you find freedom in release, as the sea does.

Visualization
Storm Watcher

At the head of the storm, storeys-high waves crash into the harbour's thick stone walls and each other. Thrown in the thrill of release, all spiked peaks and shattering explosions, a natural fireworks display.

As the tide begins to ebb, their power shifts. No longer wildly battering, hemmed in by restrictive boundaries, or caught in a battle of wills between ingoing and outgoing waves, their vast energy releases into clear space. They stretch toward freedom.

As the tideline retreats, the waves find their natural shape. They can rise without a battle, and dance freely with the wind. Even as they retreat, they reach forward.

Affirmation

I release to move forward, as the waves do.

Journal Prompts

Become curious about what may be holding you back or blocking your way forward. Can you identify any unhelpful beliefs, fears, behaviours, relationships, objects or other things that may be limiting your progress toward your intention?

What do I need to release in order to move forward?

_____

_____

_____

_____

_____

_____

_____

_____

_____

_____

_____

_____

_____

And what is my first step toward that today?

Courage

The sea wills you to see your strength in every wave that breaks in your path. It proves your resilience with challenges to extend your courage, stroke by stroke. It asks how far you will go in pursuit of yourself, toward all you can become.

When many people start sea swimming, they're scared to swim more than a few strokes away from the shore. But when they focus on their immediate goal – to put their face in the water, to swim just a few metres more, to find self-compassion for their fear – they discover just enough courage to move forward.

Each small brave action we take leaves a tiny sparkling proof to inspire us onward – a glinting sand eel in murky waters. Each builds momentum for the next. A shoal of brave lights in the dark, guiding us on.

We can't experience courage without fear, and we can't be courageous all the time. Like the sea, sometimes we roar, and sometimes we quietly persist. But both fear and courage show us what we care about – the dreams we're prepared to swim toward, or release.

True courage is wiser than the ancient "fight or flight" response to powering through danger. It aligns your bravest actions with your deepest values and purpose. Instead of racing into the fight, it first asks what it is that you are fighting for.

Sometimes courage is about saying no, making hard choices and setting boundaries. Sometimes it's knowing that you need to stop and rest, or find a safe space to be vulnerable and scared. It's courageous to be kind to yourself when your mind – and the world around you – is pushing you in another direction. In tending to your fear, you tend to your courage. And compassion for yourself and others can motivate the bravest of actions.

When you feel fearful, offer your fear compassion. Bring your focus to the wave immediately in front of you. Breathe in just enough courage to sustain you through that. And let go, allowing the wave to crash past.

Then . . . breathe in just enough courage for the next.

Blessing

May your courage and compassion
always rise to meet the waves.

Affirmation

I am courageous, whatever the ocean brings.

DIP A TOE INTO COURAGE

Head to a cold sea, or prepare a small bowl or sink of cold water.

*Take three deep breaths. Call in courage with your inhale,
and release fear with your exhale.*

*Imagine that you are about to step into a cold sea. Continue
breathing in courage and releasing fear as you place your hands in
cold water, then bring them to your face or the back of your neck.*

*Keep breathing as you adjust to the sensations.
Witness your courage. Offer yourself compassion.*

DIVE DEEPER INTO COURAGE

What could I do with just five minutes of courage?

_____

_____

_____

_____

_____

_____

And what courageous step will I take today?

_____

_____

_____

_____

_____

_____

_____

Guided Journaling Journey

Read the Theme introduction, then try the "Dip a Toe" activity to bring you consciously into the experience of letting go of fear and stepping into courage. Considering the change you want to make, use these journal prompts to reflect on how courage can support you to move forward toward your intention.

What evidence can I uncover of my past courage (both big and small moments)?

_____

_____

_____

_____

_____

_____

_____

_____

_____

_____

_____

_____

_____

What inspired me to find courage in those moments?

With this current challenge, what am I afraid of?

How much of that fear is rooted in a present reality?

_____

_____

_____

_____

_____

_____

_____

And where does the rest of the fear come from?

_____

_____

_____

_____

_____

_____

_____

_____

What would help me to face this fear?

What's the smallest courageous action I can imagine that will move me forward?

_____

_____

_____

_____

_____

_____

And the next?

_____

_____

_____

_____

_____

_____

As I step into my courage, what becomes possible?

_____

_____

_____

_____

_____

_____

_____

And how can I tend to my courage with compassion?

_____

_____

_____

_____

_____

_____

_____

Heard

The sea can push you to endure, to tread water, to fight for survival. Yet in the depths of struggle lies the courage to speak out and ask for help.
In sharing your lessons, and accepting an open hand toward calmer waters, your strength touches all.

There is a thrill in swimming in a slightly choppy sea. But when the waves reach higher than expected, or rocks rise suddenly in your path, those seas can become too challenging to face alone.

Speaking your truth and asking for help can be difficult. It's hard to share how you're feeling; to turn to others when you don't know if they will be able to support you, and to ask for what you need. You can't control how your stories will be received, but you can choose where and when you speak them.

When you haven't yet found a safe space to be heard, turn to the sea. The ocean will always hold whatever you need to share, however imperfectly you share it. Heard by the sea, you begin to hear yourself. To listen for what lies in between the lines – in the quiet and the lows. To be both the audience and the hero.

Sometimes, we don't want to share our stories – even with the water. Perhaps because we believe that in sharing them, they become real. But in speaking your experience, you begin to define how your story will be told, and where it will lead you. You shape the narrative, becoming the captain of your own ship.

Everyone feels lost in the ocean at some point. But just like the seas that travel between distant islands, our stories connect us. The more you are heard by those who truly listen (including yourself), the more possible it becomes to speak. In being heard, you begin to let go.

Your stories guide others. And in making sense of your journey, you can navigate a new path forward.

Blessing
May your voice be heard across the oceans.

Affirmation
My truth is heard above the seas.

DIP A TOE INTO HEARD

*Offer yourself compassionate touch,
like placing a hand on your heart.*

*Take a deep breath and audibly sigh as you exhale, releasing
tension. With each sigh, visualize a wave breaking and washing
away all you want to release. Repeat for a minute or so.*

Ask: **What do I need to be heard?**

*Speak aloud what needs to be heard, imagining
you're talking to the ocean.*

*Return to sighing and visualizing the wave. Connect to the
feeling of being physically supported, and heard.*

DIVE DEEPER INTO HEARD

What do I need to be heard on this journey,
why, and who do I want to hear it?

_____

_____

_____

_____

_____

_____

_____

And what first step could I take toward that today?

_____

_____

_____

_____

_____

_____

Mindful Practice
Deep Sighs

In this somatic breathing practice, you will gently
release an emotion, sigh by sigh.

So much can be expressed with a deep sigh.
It allows suffering to be witnessed, released and healed,
and is one of the body's most crucial reflexes.

As you sigh, you bring your breathing and your body
back into equilibrium, inhaling fresh oxygen and releasing waste
carbon dioxide. It's a powerful reset, one that empties your lungs
much more effectively than a shallow breath. Listening to
the sound of your sigh also echoes the sound of the sea,
offering comfort and connection.

If it's hard to identify a particular emotion or sensation,
try reading the "Ocean Exhale" poem aloud (pages 92–93).
If you wish, you can sigh between each verse, and imagine
each of these emotions leaving you one by one.

Start by bringing your attention to a minor emotional discomfort – just a 1 or 2 on an emotional scale of 10. Perhaps you're feeling frustrated about a small mistake, or just a bit tired and achy.

Name your emotions and sensations. Choose one emotion and focus on sensing this in your body, without judgement.

Take a deep breath in, hold it briefly, and then let it go with a deep sigh: feeling a full-body release. Continue sighing as you bring your attention to where you can sense the particular emotion within you. Imagine your sigh bringing gentle release to this area, little by little.

You might place your hand there, or stroke this part of your body downwards. You might tense as you inhale, and release as you exhale.

You might try visualizing your sigh as a flow of water passing through you, energetically cleansing, soothing and softening. Or simply bring your attention to the sound.

After a few minutes, bring to mind a dear friend or loved one. Imagine that they have heard your sigh, and want to offer you some words of encouragement. Imagine what they might say to you, then try to receive their compassionate words, even if this feels a little strange at first.

Reconnect to the emotion that you identified at the start of the practice. **Has your physical or emotional state shifted in any way?**

Space

The open sea extends to a vast horizon. A view that offers infinite spaciousness – a blank canvas beyond, above and below. Between here and the skyline, your scope can widen; you can move without restriction, take up space and be free.

hat do you imagine when you think about a spacious life? Time to spend by the sea? Space to do the things that you love, with the people that you love? To dally? To nurture that special spark that lies within you, and to follow your dreams? Or something else?

Modern life puts us permanently on high alert – in a "red mind" state. Bombarded with information, "urgent" needs and calls to overextend ourselves – there's simply too much information coming in for our brains to manage.

Even when we think we're multitasking, our brains are just shifting from one task to another in sequence, a cognitive process that leaves even less space in our minds.

Yet when you're by the sea, everything else falls away. You let go, releasing any need to race on to the next thing. You find space to move beyond the immediate constraints of place and time, to sense an entire lifespan.

The immensity of the landscape offers up each tiny yet significant moment still to be lived between here and the horizon. And you can sense the ripples that continue beyond and around you; the infinite directions in which you could move.

The sea reminds you that you *are* the space. All you need do is pause and breathe.

When life is busy, it's more important than ever to create space to step into. To listen to your body; to meet your emotional needs. The more often you do that, the more spacious life feels. And the more possible it is to create change.

Blessing
May the sea clear space for you to journey onward,
with freedom and purpose.

Affirmation
As I let go, I create space.

DIP A TOE INTO SPACE

Take five breaths.

As you inhale, imagine creating a little more space within your ribcage, then your belly.

As you exhale, imagine emptying your mind, creating space there too.

Set a three-minute timer and focus on clearing one small area in your immediate eyeline: perhaps a surface, a shelf, a pile of paperwork. Feel the energy of letting go and clearing space.

Reflect, witnessing your impact.

DIVE DEEPER INTO SPACE

What shifts when I create more space for this journey?

_____

_____

_____

_____

_____

And how could I do that today?

_____

_____

_____

_____

_____

_____

Ocean Ritual
To Create Space: Beach Clearing

In this ritual, you will honour and clear a space in nature, shifting energy and inviting in hope. Taking even the smallest of actions toward positive change can empower and galvanize wider change within ourselves and beyond.

A mini beach clean – removing at least three bits of manmade beach debris after every swim – can quickly become a daily ritual. It may seem just a drop in the ocean, but it ripples out. Imagine that every day, you clear. The more you clear, the more you begin to notice what is out of place. Others join you on their regular walks. You share your finds in conversation, on social media, in work you create – inspiring others. Slowly, together, we tend to our shared home, and space expands. A tiny ritual creates a sea change.

This simple practice, consciously undertaken with love for the natural world, fosters an internal shift from despondency or inertia toward hope, gratitude and compassion. As we create space for the ocean to thrive, we also create space within ourselves: a fertile landscape for new things to grow.

If you can't get to the ocean, try clearing a space elsewhere in nature, or a space in your home.

Identify the specific area that you would like to clear. Mark this out physically, or by visualizing or describing this area.

Set an intention to lovingly clear and create space – within and without.

Clear the space, bringing your mindful awareness to your impact as you do so.

Let the conscious flow and focus of this activity gently clear your mind.

When it wanders, bring your thoughts back to this vision of making change; of clearing and creating space; of tending to the ocean that you love.

When you have finished clearing the area, take a moment to pause, reflect and appreciate the shift.

What looks different?

What has been created?

What is now possible?

What did you learn from the experience?

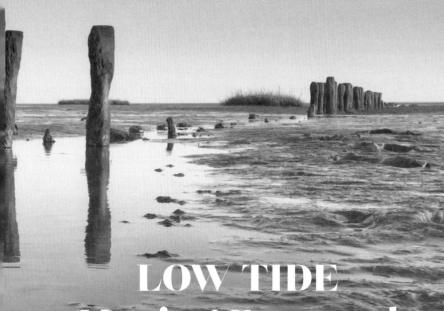

LOW TIDE
Moving Forward

OCEAN MANTRA:

With a wild ocean spirit, and a bold leap in,

limitless waves of change begin.

OCEAN DAUGHTER

Ocean daughter, in the water,

thanks the storm for all it taught her.

Honours all that waves have brought her.

Laughs that shame has still not caught her.

Rises, fierce as the past that fought her.

Boldly claims the soul that sought her.

Ocean daughter, of the water,

stretches from her ocean altar:

wild, untamed, a beach before her.

LOW TIDE

At low tide, the only way is forward. All is laid bare here – your treasures, your truths, and the rocks in your path. Land and sea map the lessons of your past and the possibilities of your future; and the distant horizon calls you onward toward change.

Moving Forward

For centuries, the sea has ignited imaginations, inspired creativity and emboldened adventurers to explore new worlds. It has also been a source of fear, fierce battles and devastating loss.

As you meet inevitable obstacles, it's only human to lose faith in your own capacity and power at times. To struggle to find a way through, to question your path, and to consider giving up.

But even at the lowest of tides, the ocean continues to flow. You can still sense the distant waves, and feel the ground thrumming beneath your feet. This Theme encourages you to look ahead and envision your next steps forward, beyond obstructions. It offers inspiration for when you feel stuck, for when unexpected challenges block your path, and you're too exhausted to progress.

With every gully carved between the rocks, the sea calls you to find a new way, to envision a fresh channel toward your wildest dreams. From the distance, the waves call you to persist – to travel onward toward the change you wish to make. To commit to your direction, explore your next stretch, and stay curious. Trusting that the turning tide will soon lift you on your way, wave by gentle wave.

Blessing

May an ocean current draw you onward.

Visualization
Beachcomber

Damp sand holds the last of this morning's sea like a sponge, squelching between your toes. The beach is vast. A flat shining plain from here to the far white lines of the breakers, peppered with pebbles and a scattered alphabet of lugworm curls.

Amongst them, treasures glimmer. Egg cases that once nurtured catfish are pocketed as mythical mermaid's purses. Marooned nurdles are picked free from stranded jellyfish tentacles. Sand-smoothed shells, cool to touch, are turned in your palm, and sea-glass marbles raised to the light.

At the lowest of tides, the sea's innermost secrets are revealed. You can stand in the ocean's naked underbelly, breathing freely on land that was once underwater. Trace the lines of limpet trails – reminders not to revisit, but move on. See the broken spines of shipwrecks – their carcasses long scavenged, yet adventure still clinging to their bones. The salt-pickled remains of ancient tree trunks – fertile woodlands that once connected the island to the shore. And an archipelago of black rock, thrown like stepping stones to a horizon that feels closer than before.

Affirmation

I move toward my intention, wave by wave.

Journal Prompts

When change feels as distant as a breaking wave on a low tide beach, bring your focus to your next conscious step across the sand. One small movement forward, a single obstacle to overcome, an individual treasure to be found: identify the next few steps that will bring you just a little closer to your intention.

What is my next step?

And my next?

_____

_____

_____

_____

_____

_____

And my next?

_____

_____

_____

_____

_____

_____

_____

_____

Curious

*The sea is renewed in every moment,
inviting fresh exploration. It calls you
to revel in the wonder of rediscovering
the world and yourself afresh, without
expectations, assumptions or judgements.*

Children can spend hours in pursuit of a question. Incessantly counting tadpoles in rock pools, poking with awe-struck fascination at the insides of jellyfish marooned on the beach, attempting to decipher the calls of seabirds, or scanning rocks for the tell-tale curves of basking seals. We are inquisitive creatures.

But curiosity, like play, is something we often unlearn as we get older. Sometimes school bores it out of us. And sometimes we set our path in stone, believing we've already learnt enough. When we only anticipate more of the same, and limit our awareness and understanding to the "facts", we lose touch with that spirit of curiosity. As we start to doubt our value, our joy and our creative ideas. As we conform to others' expectations instead of our own. As we judge our mistakes and imperfections – and stop believing we can change. As we set the bar low, based on all that we already know – rather than all that remains to be discovered.

By revealing new treasures to inspire you, unexplored depths to dive into, or a secret low-tide path that leads to a serpentine cave, the sea reconnects you to the revitalizing force of your own curiosity. To mystery, and strangeness, and to the millions of questions available to ask and learn from every day.

When you feel stuck or you need inspiration to shape a new project, step into curiosity. Allow yourself not to know, to learn as you go, and to surprise yourself with your own creativity. Ask a question, and stay open to new answers. Because there's always more than one. You don't have to get it "right". You just need to believe that there is always more to discover.

When you approach your challenge with a curious mindset, new questions and ways of progressing reveal themselves to you.

Blessing

May you allow each breath to be a question that
uncovers treasures within you.

Affirmation

I am a curious explorer on a wild adventure.

DIP A TOE INTO CURIOUS

Hold an object that reminds you of the sea (for example, a shell, a pebble or a handful of sand) and look at it afresh, as if through the eyes of a curious child.

Observe as much as you can about the object in one minute – its feel, shape, weight, texture, patterns – and ask yourself three new questions about it.

List seven new ways you could use it. Bad ideas are absolutely fine (even to be encouraged!); this practice is simply about opening up to curiosity.

DIVE DEEPER INTO CURIOUS

What shifts when I ask different questions?

_____

_____

_____

_____

_____

_____

And what new question will I ask to move forward today?

_____

_____

_____

_____

_____

_____

_____

Guided Journaling Journey

Read the Theme introduction, then try the "Dip a Toe" activity to shift into a curious mindset. Thinking about the change you want to make, use the writing prompts below to uncover and consider new ways of seeing and responding to this.

Without thinking too hard or trying to come up with the 'best possible' answers, list seven...

1. Small steps I could take to move forward toward the change I desire today.

_____

_____

_____

_____

_____

_____

_____

_____

_____

_____

_____

2. New questions I could ask myself about this challenge, things I've learnt, am learning, or hope to learn as I explore this intention.

3. New dreams I'd like to move toward
beyond this intention.

_____

_____

_____

_____

_____

_____

_____

_____

_____

_____

_____

_____

_____

_____

_____

_____

What might I learn if I look at my current challenges from the perspective of . . .

1. Others involved in or impacted by these?

_____

_____

_____

_____

_____

_____

_____

_____

_____

_____

_____

_____

_____

_____

_____

_____

_____

2. Me, one month from now, having made a change?

_____

_____

_____

_____

_____

_____

_____

3. Me, a year from now, having progressed even further?

_____

_____

_____

_____

_____

_____

_____

_____

Now ask yourself:

1. What stories have I been telling myself about this
challenge or change?

_____

_____

_____

_____

_____

_____

_____

2. What else might be true or possible?

_____

_____

_____

_____

_____

_____

_____

3. What would I do if I knew I could not fail?

Stretch

The sea tests your willingness to extend, your capacity for movement, the limits of your endurance. It asks you to leave the safety of familiar land, and explore the space between your desire to change and your capacity to stretch into unknown territory.

The sea reminds us that everything stretches. Our bodies change; our dreams evolve; our circumstances, power and beliefs transform. As we become aware of our arrival at a particular place or experience – or an understanding of ourselves – we realize we are moving on again.

The sea flows constantly from one state to the next – it stretches, then retreats. It knows when to stretch further; and when to rest in the middle ground between moons. When you stretch, do you also make time to seek out rest and tender self-care?

Stretching yourself is not the same as being over-stretched – by pushing yourself too hard, or in response to circumstances beyond your control. When we consciously stretch into a new area – choosing a level of discomfort that allows us to grow – we are able to extend our capacity without strain. We build the flexibility and inner strength that we need to face the waves into which we reach. Stretching just a little further each time, we start to perceive our shifting edges. We move through old boundaries. We expand our reach, and become more.

Reaching beyond the familiar requires presence, courage and trust. You bring yourself into presence when you sense overwhelm and choose to take a breath instead. You find courage when you are fearful. You claim trust when you doubt, remind yourself of your intention, and take conscious onward action nonetheless.

Swim a little out of your depth, beyond the comfort zone. Allow the sea to hold you as it lifts your toes from the floor. For the reward is always more than whatever you stretch toward. It is the gift of a life lived in alignment. With clarity and purpose. In evolution and fluidity. Always open to new opportunities, falling and rising. Always learning, always stretching.

Blessing

May you reach beyond familiar shores,
with the ease of a cresting wave.

Affirmation

As I stretch, I expand. As I expand,
I welcome the oceans within me.

DIP A TOE INTO STRETCH

Divide a piece of paper into three sections by drawing two horizontal lines. Imagine that these sections mark out the sky, sea and land.

Imagine that land represents your safe ground: what you know and is familiar. Describe what's possible here right now.

On the horizon, far out to sea, name a big stretch you want to make – one that doesn't yet feel possible.

Identify your stretch zone – in the water, a little closer to the horizon, yet where you can easily return to the land. Describe what's possible here.

DIVE DEEPER INTO STRETCH

Where do I want to stretch further?

_____

_____

_____

_____

_____

_____

And how will I stretch today?

_____

_____

_____

_____

_____

_____

Mindful Practice
Mexican Wave

In a Mexican wave, a crowd raise and lower their arms, their movement rippling onward like a rising swell. In this somatic practice, you will find flow and focus as you stretch your body and embody water.

Before any exercise, we stretch to create space and flexibility, avoid injury, and expand our physical capabilities. Stretching and breathing mindfully can have a similar effect on our brains, creating space within, and shifting how we perceive ourselves and our challenge.

In this calming physical flow, you embody water, and move stagnant energy through your body. If you're unable to stand, do this exercise seated. Whatever your physical capacity, the more you understand your own shifting limits, and stretch – little by little – the further you can extend, both physically and emotionally.

Stand, taking a moment to sense the gentle hold of gravity. Observe how you feel, body and mind.

As you breathe in, raise your arms up.

As you breathe out, lower your arms in front of your body. Sense yourself as a wave, constantly rising and falling.

Continue with this simple movement for as long as feels good, finding your own rhythm. Stay mindful that your physical capacity will be different each day. You may choose to keep your movements small. Or to stretch further, bending your knees, bringing your hands to the floor, before rising up on tiptoes to reach to the sky. You may find a sense of momentum that energizes you, or allow your breath and movements to slow and deepen.

When your mind wanders, bring yourself back to the sound of your breath. To the physical sensations of the movement, the experience of flow, and your shifting capacity to stretch.

As you approach the end of your practice, slowly reduce the scale of your stretch. Bring your hands to your heart. Feel the flow continuing with your breath.

Notice how you feel having completed this practice.

Has anything shifted, physically or emotionally?

Persist

Whether storms rage or gentle waters kiss the coast, the waves continue to the shore. The sea keeps moving, whether or not you choose to swim. Always rising and resting, rising and resting.
One wave at a time.

atching the ocean, you are reminded that each wave is fleeting. This life you have, right now – with all of its gifts and challenges – is precious. Like the sea, it continues onward, whether or not you choose to make a change. Your time is both limited and full of possibility.

Your progress forward is as much about the rest as the rise. Each pause between the waves allows the sea to persist, the tides to turn, the waves to travel on to the shore. Those quiet troughs only deepen the reach of the peaks. As conditions change, the scale and pace of the waves shifts in response. Sometimes a tiny ripple, sometimes a crashing surge – but always that dance between rising and resting.

Perhaps most importantly of all, each wave rolling onward has a clear direction – to the shore, or back to the sea. To persevere, you need the same clarity. About both the destination you're moving toward, and the forces that propel you on this journey: your reason for making this change or facing this challenge.

Reconnect to your values, to what you love, and to why you began this journey. Why does this matter? Describe and visualize what you hope to move toward – the bright new shores to which this sea change is leading you. How will it feel to be on the other side of this ocean? What will you do, see or experience differently there?

Tend to this vision of your destination, refreshing and revisiting it: this is your inspiration to persist.

Blessing

May you persevere as the swell rises,
as the tides turn, in pursuit of all you can be.

Affirmation

Like a rising swell, I persist.

DIP A TOE INTO PERSISTENCE

*Breathe in, counting to four. Pause for a brief moment.
Then breathe out for a count of four. Pause again.*

*Explore slightly extending the length of your exhale,
and the length of your pauses between each breath.*

*Don't strain or overextend; this practice should feel
comfortable and ease-filled.*

*Notice how your breath continues ever onward like waves.
How a pause can clear your mind and bring focus.*

*Return to breathing normally, and consider your destination on this
journey:* **What images, words or feelings come to mind?**

DIVE DEEPER INTO PERSISTENCE

Where am I headed and why?

_____

_____

_____

_____

_____

_____

And how can I connect to that today?

_____

_____

_____

_____

_____

_____

Ocean Ritual
To Inspire Perseverance: Sea Glass, the Sea and Me

In this ritual, you will visualize the transformation of sea glass over time while reflecting on your own journey. Sea glass reminds us that what was once broken or discarded can be reshaped, rediscovered and appreciated anew: a journey of transformation that echoes your own.

Set an intention: to seek guidance from sea glass and the sea.

As you search the beach for sea glass, take a moment to observe the sea and the waves' persistence. If you're at home, you could watch a film of the ocean and use an old piece of sea glass for this ritual.

Once you have found a piece of sea glass that calls to you, hold this in your hand and deeply consider it: its appearance, weight and energy.

Close your eyes and imagine or attune to the journey it has made to reach you. You can visualize, speak or write this down, or explore it through movement.

Notice the highs and lows, the moments of stillness and flow, the modes of transformation. Sense its travel from ancient rocks to sand fired as glass, becoming something new. The lives it touched, the purposes it served, the moment of breakage. Its journey to the ocean, to be turned and changed by the waves. Arriving on the beach, to be found by you.

Observe your sea glass afresh as you repeat this mantra:

As I journey, my beauty and resilience are revealed.

*Still holding the sea glass, now connect to the sea in which
the glass was transformed over time. Sense the dance between
the two; the energy and persistence of the ocean, sculpting
and flowing, moving and shaping.*

Repeat the previous mantra and add another:

As I persevere, I shape my life.

*Finally, bring your current challenge to mind, and sense
the journey that you have already made to arrive here.
All that has shaped you, and all that you have shaped.
Connect to your capacity to enact change.*

Complete your ritual by repeating the mantras, and offering thanks.

*Reflect on the experience and consider how this might help
you to move forward.*

*Later, whenever you need to connect to your capacity to persist
and transform, hold the sea glass, and repeat the mantras.*

RISING TIDE
Gratitude and Awe

We do not need to earn the wonder of the sea,

for like our spirit, she is free.

TO THE SEA,
FOR EVERYTHING

Thank you seems inadequate:

a raindrop in an ocean.

But what could be more beautiful

than water motes in motion?

RISING TIDE

As the tide rises, the sea flows toward you, bearing gifts. In the ocean's approach, there is both ease and wonder. Possibilities unfurl at your feet, teasing you into joy and bringing you into flow: you and the sea, rising together.

Gratitude and Awe

Gratitude brings us into the present, while awe expands our perception – of time, of what's possible, and of ourselves. Both experiences can transform the way we feel and relate to others, how we see the world, and how we take action.

As you move toward change, nurture both gratitude and awe. Follow your bliss. Delight in all the gifts to be found around and within you. Feel each soft step upon the sand, each warm sunbeam on your skin, each gift of salt on your tongue. Leave daily footprints of thankfulness for the sea to wash away.

When the waves are high and you can barely see the sky, trust to awe. When your dams tumble, laugh and marvel at your learning. Let the ocean put problems into perspective, and connect you to life's most thrilling new possibilities.

For each moment of wonder and gratitude cultivates a nascent spring of joy within you. With tender care, that spring becomes a stream, a waterfall, a river and, eventually, an ocean. As joy rises within you, it propels you forward, and ripples out to others.

In this Theme, you are reminded to receive life's gifts, and to invite in playfulness and creativity to support and inspire you. You are called to step into universal flow, awakening faith in your capacity to overcome challenges – and in your own magic.

Blessing

May joy and wonder rise within you,
and power you onward.

Visualization
Summer Shores

*The horizon is a bobbing bunting of white sails on a steady line.
The sky a fathomless blue. A space of infinite cobalt, brimming with
galaxies, rippling close enough to touch. As if one could hang wind
chimes and whirling mobiles on every unseen star, spin the
crescent moon, and swim through blue to eternity.*

*At your feet, the siren sounds of glinting waves sigh ever closer.
Each unfurling breaker a momentary lens, framing rippling rainbows
and darting fish. Bubbles pop like perfect pancakes, soft foam
clearing your footsteps. Laughing families gather towels and shoes,
chase toddlers toward dry sand. Two remain, stoic in a sandcastle
fort, poised to dam the sea. As waves breach the walls,
they squeal with delight, accepting defeat with joy.*

*These precious moments. Each footstep taken, never to be
taken again. Wonder all around you, gifts beyond measure:
the ocean with an open heart.*

Affirmation

The sea inspires me to journey further.

Journal Prompts

Think about all that inspires you. All that brings you joy. All that empowers you to pursue your deepest dreams. Consider how you might call on some of these things, people, places and practices as you move toward your intention.

What will inspire me to journey further?

And how could I bring that into my day today?

Receive

The wonder of the sea is not earned or deserved. It is an offering, given and received without constraint. A constant presence that offers you the choice: to deny your innate worthiness and resist the gift, or to accept it in gratitude.

hen we head to the sea, it offers us exactly what we need. Soothing peace or courageous vitality, a battle to find truth or acceptance, or a burst of epic beauty, the possibilities are endless, and ever-evolving.

When you are open to receiving whatever comes, the sea will offer you a gift. And time spent by the sea – or envisioning it as you do here – will shift you into a more receptive state. One in which you can appreciate all that is available to you in each moment. Where you can listen without judgement, discern what matters, sense what you really need – and call it in. Where you can hear both the ocean's guidance for you and your own intuition.

To receive, all you need do is believe you are worthy of the gift – and of sharing your own gifts with others. Like the sea, you are constantly in flow, giving and receiving – a reciprocal exchange. You breathe in before you breathe out. You offer, and you receive. Just as each wave responds to forces that drive it forward, and the pull of gravity that draws it back.

Where are you in this flow right now? Perhaps you're giving more – offering support and guidance, meeting responsibilities, putting others' needs ahead of your own? Or perhaps you're receiving support and finding it hard to give. Wherever you find yourself, you are always worthy of receiving, and there is always a gift to give in return. Your appreciation, your presence, your open heart. An opportunity to experience human connection or thankfulness.

Taking a couple of minutes to notice and appreciate all that you receive each day – even when that's hard – is more than just a powerful gratitude practice. It's also a tool for shifting perspective, creating energetic flow, and inviting more gifts into your life.

Blessing
May you witness, accept and delight in
the ocean's many gifts.

Affirmation
I am worthy of the sea's gifts.

DIP A TOE INTO RECEIVE

*Listen to the sounds of the sea. If you wish, listen to a recording
of ocean sounds and bring your attention within.
Or listen for this sound in your breath. You might even
hold a shell to your ear as children do.*

*As your mind wanders, guide your attention gently
back to the sound of the sea, without judgement. Just like
a wave washes footprints from the sand, let the sea clear
distracting thoughts from your mind as they arise.*

*When you feel calm, grounded and open,
ask the sea for guidance. Repeat this mantra:*

I am ready to receive.

I am worthy to receive.

I am open to receive.

Listen to what comes.

*For some additional guidance, choose a blessings
or oracle card.*

DIVE DEEPER INTO RECEIVE

What shifts when I open to receive?

_____

_____

_____

_____

_____

And what do I want to invite in today?

_____

_____

_____

_____

_____

_____

Guided Journaling Journey

Read the Theme introduction, then try the "Dip a Toe" activity to awaken your capacity to receive. Consider the change you want to make. Now use the writing prompts below to become clearer about what you would like to give and receive on this journey, and to understand more deeply the gifts available to you.

What do I love to give?

What do I love to receive?

_____

_____

_____

_____

_____

_____

_____

What is hard to give?

_____

_____

_____

_____

_____

_____

_____

_____

What is hard to receive?

What are the greatest gifts I have ever received?

_____

_____

_____

_____

_____

_____

What are the greatest gifts I have ever given?

_____

_____

_____

_____

_____

_____

_____

What gifts have I already received today?

_____

_____

_____

_____

_____

_____

_____

_____

_____

_____

_____

_____

_____

_____

_____

_____

What gifts do I have (within and without) that will support me to make this change or pursue this intention?

_____

_____

_____

_____

_____

_____

_____

_____

_____

_____

_____

_____

_____

_____

_____

_____

_____

What gifts would I like to receive as a result of making this change?

_____

_____

_____

_____

_____

_____

_____

What gifts am I already receiving as I move toward change?

_____

_____

_____

_____

_____

_____

_____

_____

Play

The sea beckons to joyful children, ageless in the water. It is a gleeful promise of unconstrained fun, free of self-consciousness and judgement. Embracing play, you reject limits, open up to the new, learn and grow.

The sea has the power to remind us of the children we once were – or that we dreamt of being. It calls us to reconnect to the deeply felt exhilaration of running to the water's edge. Piling up sand castles until they collapse. Freely making stick-marks in the sand. Plunging elbow-deep into a pool to tickle a fish. Sifting sand between our fingers, or kicking water high into the air. Vast expanses of freedom and joy, surfing a vibrant flow of games, imagination and invention.

Whether or not you had that experience as a child, your inner child still craves time to play, create, experiment and have fun. Time without rules, restrictions or fixed outcomes. Time to be joyful and light-hearted, without fear of judgement or being "good enough". That's how we expanded our perception of the world as children. And how we grow and move forward as adults.

Sometimes, facing a change or a challenge, we take it all too seriously. If we become fixed on one plan, structure or way of doing things – and that doesn't work out – we can become despondent, overly analytical, or lost. We can struggle to come up with creative solutions and fluid responses. We forget that there is more to life. And that delight can inspire us forward.

When that happens, put everything down and play. Ask yourself where you find your fun and joy these days. And what your inner child really wants from you today – to play on the beach, make art, or something else?

Blessing

May you feel the glee of a welcoming sea
on golden sands.

Affirmation

I follow my bliss, and dance with the waves.

DIP A TOE INTO PLAYFULNESS

*Take a few deep ocean breaths, and connect
to that child within you.*

*To help, you might use a photo of yourself as a child,
or an image of a child at play.*

*Imagine this child playing happily on the beach.
You might visualize this scene in your mind or describe
it in your journal.*

*Tell your inner child about your challenge or the
change you want to make, and listen to whatever
guidance they have to share.*

DIVE DEEPER INTO PLAYFULNESS

What shifts on this journey when I am playful?

_____

_____

_____

_____

_____

_____

And how will I play today?

_____

_____

_____

_____

_____

_____

Mindful Practice
Ocean Art

In this practice, you will create an ocean-inspired artwork on the beach or at home as a playful way to step into creative flow.

If you can't get to the sea, *try making an ocean collage instead. Intuitively cut out magazine pictures or words – choosing those that capture how the sea makes you (or your inner child) feel.*

Arrange your images on a sheet of paper. Step back and consider the reflection questions opposite.

You might like to display your collage as a reminder of how the sea makes you feel, and of your capacity to play and connect to the ocean.

If you can get to the sea, *gather materials from the beach – collect whatever catches your eye. Pebbles, shells, sand, seaweed, plastic debris, whatever the sea offers.*

Arrange what you've found into an artwork.

You might draw in the sand, make a shape or an image, a symbol or a word, a structure, an abstract picture, or something completely different.

Notice the textures, colours and shapes. Let your inner child and your intuition guide you. You can't do this "wrong" or "badly" – it's all play.

Step back and reflect.

What do you see?

How was the experience, and what might you learn from that?

Is there anything in your artwork that relates to your current challenge?

Magic

Where light enters the sea, there is glorious alchemy. Like light, wherever you enter the world, you create your own magic. Conjuring the sun and the moon – being and soul – into the shifting ritual of the tides, the sea invokes your own innate capacity to synthesize, transform, and call in.

The more time you spend with the sea, the more you start to sense its magic. In sunrises and sunsets. In the shining black eyes of a seal, or the glimpsed silver shiver of a fish. In a cluster of pale limpets against dark rock, a heart stone at your feet, or a falling white feather that ripples a silent rock pool.

You slowly start to understand that you too are made of that same magic. That the magic flows from the sea to you and back again. That it flows through all of us. You begin to make rituals of moments, and find meaning in nature's signs. You seek out connections between the shifting landscape and your own soul knowing. You celebrate with gratitude and awe each rumbling wave that lifts you onward. And as you step bravely into action, attuned to the sea, you step into universal flow.

As you claim your magic – tend to it and share it – you connect to a force beyond your own: an energetic ocean that guides you through changes and challenges toward a greater purpose. It asks you to loosen constraints and fixed ideas, to seek out fluidity and hidden depths; to trust in love.

Of course, like waves and tides, your sense of magic ebbs and flows. It's always there, but sometimes it's harder to believe in. There are days when it feels like you could almost touch it. And others when you can barely glimpse the idea of magic, let alone grasp your own. Don't be disheartened. Offer your magic tender care through the crashing waves and roaring storms – keep calling it in, listening, sensing, and trusting it to guide you when the time is right.

When you use your magic to restore the health of the ocean, you align ever more deeply with its flow. You uncover your role in life's great unfolding. In the sea's wisdom and miracles, you discover the magic that connects us all. In healing the sea, we heal each other.

Blessing

May you deepen your faith in the sea,
and trust in the power of your own magic.

Affirmation

I hold an ocean of magic within me.

DIP A TOE INTO MAGIC

Set an intention to seek out magic. To open to guidance from the sea and your inner knowing.

Turn the pages of this journal and notice which image or words draw your attention.

Pause there, and connect to what you find.

Seek out a message for yourself in this moment, trusting that universal flow will bring the insight you need.

DIVE DEEPER INTO MAGIC

What shifts when I trust in my own magic?

_____

_____

_____

_____

_____

_____

And where is it guiding me today?

_____

_____

_____

_____

_____

_____

_____

Ocean Ritual
To Awaken Your Ocean Magic: Ocean Energy Flow

In this ritual, you will visualize a magical flow of cleansing
and invigorating ocean energy.

You can do this meditation on the seashore,
or visualize this scene at home by imagining yourself
sat at the water's edge tasting the sea spray in the air;
or sat peacefully at the bottom of a calm ocean.

*Begin with Ocean Breath (page 30)
or Tidal Breaths (page 42) to bring yourself into a
peaceful state as you bring the sea to mind.*

*Raise your arms, palms facing but apart,
as if creating a funnel above yourself.*

Speak your intention: **I open to the ocean's magic.**

*Imagine the ocean's energy starting to flow down
between your open arms with the soothing
quality of water.*

*Sense the flow travelling through the top of your head to
your neck, shoulders, chest, arms, all the way down your spine.
On through your belly, pelvis and sacrum, through your
legs and feet to the earth.*

*Imagine it flowing onward, grounding and connecting
you to the shore or ocean floor on which you sit. Flowing through
you and on into the sea.*

*Bringing your attention to each part of your body in turn, notice
where the flow feels ease-filled. If it feels stuck, pause in that area
without judgement, and offer yourself love and compassion,
repeating your intention.*

*You might sense a softening of these blocks, like sand
giving way – or the water may simply find a path to flow around
these for now. Allow the flow to carry anything
that needs to be released to the ocean.*

*As you sense a path clearing within, and the ocean's
magic flowing freely, you might choose to gently increase
the flow, inviting in more energy if that feels nurturing.*

*When you feel ready, open your arms wider, sensing your
connection to the horizon and the ocean surface.*

*Now visualize yourself sharing this magic with the sea, rippling
it out around you, in whatever way feels good.*

*To finish the ritual, bring your arms together above
your head. Then bring your hands to your heart,
offering thanks to the ocean.*

End by repeating the mantra: **I am magic. We are one.**

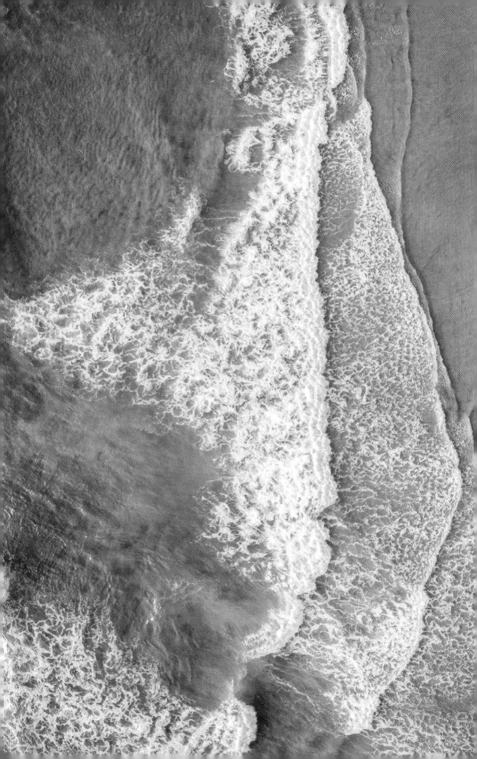

May You Journey With the Sea

In the quiet and the roar, the sea is always talking to you, bearing truths across the water with the power to touch and open your ocean heart. It is a steady yet ever-changing presence that both grounds and lifts. A luminous space that shows you who and what you are, where you came from, and what you could become.

As you have journeyed through this journal, the sea has called you to seek out self-compassion, to let go of the things that hold you back, to witness the beauty of your life, and to find new ways to inspire yourself forward – even when that's difficult.

Hand in hand with the ocean, you have stepped into presence, into kindness and expansiveness. Sought out the courage to change, to be heard, and to make space. You have become curious about how, why and when you persevere, and stretched into and beyond your edges. You have opened to receive what comes, found a playfulness in creativity, and started to explore your own magic and universal flow.

As you journey on, trust in your own capacity to embody the ocean's lessons, even as the tides shift. Be water, flowing ever onward. Seek ways to nurture and protect the oceans: both the seas that flow within you, and those more tangible oceans across the world that offer us such deep inspiration. Allow this journal to be a reminder of your heart connection to the sea, the holder of your ocean truths and possibilities, and the gathering momentum that propels you forward, toward a better world.

May you be loved

May you be nourished

May you know the gifts of the sea

About the Author

PIPPA BEST is a certified Blue Health Coach™, ocean advocate, passionate sea swimmer, and founder of nature wellness company Sea Soul Blessings.

At Sea Soul Blessings, she creates mindful compassionate resources that connect us more deeply to the sea, and to ourselves – so that together, we can be the change that the world needs.

As a life and career coach, freelance writer and script editor, Pippa has spent more than 25 years asking others (and herself) the right question at the right moment – and holding space for the answers. Trusting in intuition, self-compassion and the sea's guidance has transformed her own life for the better in every way. This experience lies at the heart of all that she shares in this journal, at ocean retreats by the sea in Cornwall, and in her online community.

Pippa is also the creator of the Sea Soul Journeys Oracle Cards. Find out more at www.seasoulblessings.com.

Acknowledgements

For an ocean of love, Carn, Jago, Loveday, Penny and JB, Anna and Brian.

For the soul-sustaining encouragement, Kari, Pippa, Angela, Tiana, my morning swim gang, the Blue Health Coach community and my amazing synchro sisters, Out of Sink.

For the insights and editing, Jo Lal, Sue Lascelles and Beth Bishop.

For support along the way, Cultivator Cornwall.

For forming the sea that shaped the seaglass of this journal – Hiro Boga, Johann Hari, Lizzi Larabalestier, Kristin Neff, Hannah Marcotti, Wallace J. Nichols, Thich Nhat Hahn, Leif Olsen, Andréa Ranae, all the generations that came before, and all those beautiful souls in the Sea Circle.

Thank you each and every one.